D0045854

# MORALS
# FOR
# MANKIND

# MORALS
# FOR
# MANKIND

HERBERT W. SCHNEIDER

The Paul Anthony Brick Lectures
Inaugural Series
1960

*University of Missouri Press* • *Columbia*

# *Foreword*

THE Paul Anthony Brick Lectureship was established by the Board of Curators of the University of Missouri as a memorial to the man whose name it bears. Mr. Brick was not a native Missourian, nor was he an alumnus of the University of Missouri; he graduated from the University of Nebraska, majoring in chemistry, and spent many years as a foreign representative of the International Harvester Company. At the time of his death, March 1, 1948, he lived in Buffalo, Missouri, where he had resided for about twenty years. In his will Mr. Brick bequeathed a generous amount to the University of Missouri. Inquiry from the lawyer who administered his estate elicited the information that Mr. Brick gave this money "for the sole reason that he liked the State of Missouri and wanted his money to go for educational purposes."

The specifications in Mr. Brick's will indicated only that he wished his money "to be used to develop the science of ethics." Since bequests with so few restrictions are somewhat rare in university circles, a careful attempt was made to provide for the use of the money in accordance with the spirit of Mr. Brick's wishes. As a result the Paul Anthony Brick Lectureship was established. This provides for a series of three lectures on ethics to be given at the University of Missouri annually, or possibly biennially, as suitable speakers become available. The stipulations are that the lectures "shall be designed for the general audience, but shall be scholarly in content, and shall be given by men who have an established reputation for competence in the field. The subject-matter of the lectureship shall be determined broadly, including ethics not merely in the technical and philosophical sense but also in its relations to literature, society, religion, and other phases of contemporary culture." The fund provides also for the publication of each series of lectures.

The committee administering the lectureship considers itself very fortunate that this series was inaugurated by Dr. Herbert Wallace Schneider. Eminently prepared by his many years of teaching philosophy and religion at Columbia University, and by his wide experience in UNESCO, he is well qualified to speak on the problem of how moral bonds may unite peoples of different cultures. His lectures, under the title "Morals for Mankind," were given at the University of Missouri, March 23-24, 1960, and the committee is proud to present to the public this inaugural volume in which the lectures are published substantially as given. The response to Dr. Schneider's lectures was enthusiastic, and the committee feels that the present volume, together with the assurance of the publication of ensuing volumes in the series, will provide an opportunity for the public to learn something about the important social and moral problems of our times, and how the most eminent authorities propose to clarify them.

A. CORNELIUS BENJAMIN
*Chairman, Brick Committee*

# *Preface*

PAUL ANTHONY BRICK'S conviction, derived from years of practical experience and of devotion to public affairs, that there is an urgent need for a better conception of the science of ethics was clearly with him not an academic exercise but the reflection of a deep, personal concern. In calling attention to this need, he anticipated a general public concern for the state of morals throughout the world. Whether it be due to man's ignorance of moral truth or to his ineffective application of common knowledge, there is obviously something very wrong about the present condition of human affairs. And it is the public duty of professional moralists, in or out of school, to make a more intensive and informative diagnosis of mankind's critical illness. The series of lectures which Mr. Brick has endowed should serve to stimulate scientific research in a field where research is still groping among problems too baffling for its meager resources and too urgent for calm reflection. It would be gratifying if the lectures could also report from time to time some tangible signs of enlightenment and practical success in coping with man's moral miseries.

This first series will certainly show that the need for ethical science is great, but it is intended to show also that the opportunities for advance in such science are at hand. It is now too late to debate the academic question whether or not there can be a science of morals; there simply *must* be such a science and it must come quickly. These three initial explorations in the series deal in a very elementary way with the basic problems; the elementary statement of the problems is far from solving them, but it may open up the field for more detailed and precise investigations. What orientation may be provided is not philosophical, for the need is not primarily philosophical. The intention behind this initial effort is to clear away verbal brush and dialectical barbed wire, so that the actual state of moral affairs may appear plainly and ready for constructive action. The mysteries have been celebrated sufficiently; it is now time for hard work. The fields are also sufficiently bloodsoaked; it is high time to make them productive of human welfare.

I wish to express my special indebtedness in preparing these lectures first of all to the generosity and hospitality of the University of Missouri which made it possible for me to concentrate on this task; then, to the stimulation provided by the Third East-West Philosophy Conference at the University of Hawaii in 1959, directed by Charles A. Moore, and by the Study Project of the Church Peace Union in the field of religious ethics. The trustees of the Blaisdell Institute of Advanced Study in World Cultures and Religions have generously granted me the use of its resources for this work, and the Institute's Secretary, Jeannette S. Griggs, has given expert assistance in the editing of the manuscript.

HERBERT W. SCHNEIDER

*Claremont, California*
*March, 1960*

# Contents

xiii

# I

## MORAL
## PRINCIPLES
## AND
## MORAL
## KNOWLEDGE

EVERY generation, since the day when Adam and Eve tried to obtain the knowledge of good and evil by tasting forbidden fruit, finds itself reopening the problem of moral knowledge. The reason is not hard to find: every generation must acquire moral experience for itself. Information can be passed on from generation to generation, but every man's conscience dies with him. No conscience that is built up on secondhand knowledge can stand up against the hard knocks that consciences usually receive in the course of a lifetime, and since a conscience to be useful must be homemade, one of the most urgent and strenuous tasks facing a growing mind is this problem of acquiring an adequate conscience for the life of a new generation.

A conscience is molded in the course of moral experience. When it first shows itself it is a bright, transparent plastic covering for innocence. With the gradual loss of innocence, as children steal more and more fruit from the tree of the knowledge of good and evil and wander into the world of social play and systematic work, the early excitement of adventure turns into an awareness of responsibilities. Consciousness of a profusion of goods and evils is gradually organized into a knowledge of types of values—among them, moral values. A conscience operates by wounding consciousness; it is working best when it is a "bad" conscience, that is, when it is registering what went wrong in the day's work or play. These pricks of conscience, which are occasionally heavy blows, gradually give it an unpleasant quality; it has nuisance value. It forces its owner to face the daily round of wrongs. But out of this daily and disagreeable acquaintance with wrongs, which is knowledge on the lowest, empirical level, there emerges the discovery of principles of right. Knowledge of evil comes to us in the form of bitter practical experiences; knowledge of the right comes later and in the form of principles. General principles, though they are the foundation of ethical science, come last in moral experience. It is this tragic fact that each generation must learn empirically. Moral knowledge comes *ex post facto* too late to be immediately useful but with a sobering effect for the future. This familiar truth implies that conscience in its infancy is quite different from conscience full grown. It begins in particular experiences of disapproval and grows into a knowledge of social and reasonable norms of conduct. Consequently our attempt to understand conscience must take account of its career from infancy to maturity; we cannot assume that it is a built-in regulator of human nature, infallibly indicating to the owner when and how he goes wrong, for conscience itself must be trained to become responsible.

There is a story in the Buddhist writings about a young man who came to a teacher and asked: "Has each body only one conscience, or may it have several?" The teacher replied, "Go home and find out for yourself." He returned later and reported: "I discovered that I have only one conscience. I could not kill it. It will not go away. I could not grasp it, for it won't stay in one's grip. I tried to pick it to pieces, but then I could not pick up the pieces. I could not get a look at it. I tried to understand it, but it appeared unintelligible. I tried to ignore it, but it wouldn't leave me. I thought it could not exist, but there it was. It is wide-awake but escapes when attended to. I am unable to say what it is."

"My dear boy," said the teacher, "you can't taste sugar by hearing about sweetness, and its taste will never enter your understanding. Only with the tongue can the taste of sugar be known. But a teacher who explains conscience to you with his tongue had better be thrown out into space."

Huckleberry Finn, in a familiar passage, sums up his similar experience with his conscience as follows: "It don't make no difference whether you do right or wrong, a person's conscience ain't got no sense, and just goes for him anyway. If I had a yaller dog that didn't know no more than a person's conscience does I would pison him. It takes up more room than all the rest of a person's insides, and yet ain't no good nohow." (Mark Twain, *Huckleberry Finn*.)

Profiting by the moral of these tales, I shall take for granted that we all live with consciences of a sort and that we have them immediately whether we understand them or not. But when it comes to *principles* of conscience, these are not given us ready-made when we get our consciences. They must be learned the hard way, and learned with social intelligence, not with the tongue.

Before I turn to the examination of social intelligence, let me say a bit about learning with the tongue. Any child, and many apparent adults, like Adam and Eve, begins by tasting whatever comes along. How else could one begin? With obedience? No, for obedience follows upon the fruits of disobedience, and disobedience is an experiment in tasting. The imperative mood in which rules are usually uttered is not in itself impressive to innocent minds. Imperatives become noteworthy to the extent that the disregarding of rules becomes unpleasant or, if not unpleasant, socially unprofitable. Hence, I repeat, tasting or testing comes first in morals.

The general result of this learning process is the emergence of what is called *good taste*. Good taste implies critical judgment. But just as tasting is always the tasting of something particular, so judgment is good taste in the particular area of experience where the tasting has been carried on. Education is the acquiring of good taste or judgment in more and more areas. It involves exposure to more and more types of tasting. If education is broad enough it generates what is commonly called an interest in the art of life. But the art of life is not a general art of living in general; it is the accumulation and interrelation of many types of good judgment gathered from the various fields of experience. A person who has acquired some critical experience in the practical arts, in some of the fine arts, in public affairs, and in a professional technique, may be said to be engaged in the liberal art of living well, and may be said to have acquired a fairly general sense of values. What he has really acquired is an ability to evaluate in the more important affairs of life. In short, this so-called sense of values is not innate. It comes from educated tasting. It is not common sense, for it is neither common nor a sense. It may begin with common sense, if education happens to begin with the common values of daily life, which is not as common an education as it is supposed to be. The sense of values is not a sense at all; values are not sensed. It is believed by many who should know better that values are immediately perceived, tasted, liked. Value-sensing, they say, is liking, for whatever is liked is a value so long as it continues to be liked. Accordingly, a man is supposed to have knowledge of values when he knows what he likes and dislikes; he is an experienced taster. Such theories overlook the difference between habitual taste and good taste. A person may be quite positive and dogmatic about his likes and dislikes and yet have no experimental interest in tasting. He would not be said to have a sense of values. Values must be discovered experimentally, for good taste is discriminating and implies that there has been testing along with tasting.

The story of Adam and Eve's tasting would be insignificant if it failed to report their tasting as a kind of learning; their eating of the apple opened their moral eyes; they learned something quite different from the taste of an apple. We are not informed whether Eve liked the apple and Adam didn't or whether both liked it or neither. In any case there was a moral worm or serpent in it. This particular tasting of an apple involved the testing of an hypothesis about knowledge. These original sinners were not interested in apples, we are told, but in the more general knowledge of good and evil. When tasting is thus a genuine experiment, it has something to do with creating a sense of values, for when there is an awareness of the interrelations among the consequences of acts of deliberate tasting, then there is the beginning of wisdom. Relating acts of tasting to each other leads to an opening of the eyes of the mind. This intellectual process, this relating of tasting to liking and then of liking to enjoying, of enjoying to satisfactions, of satisfactions to happiness, and of happiness to living well, culminates in the knowledge of principles of evaluation. A sense of values is not completely educated until it yields such principles. Principles are few and difficult to get for they are general propositions. To arrive finally at a principle is to have learned something about the general relation of tasting to testing.

So much for the elementary theory of the sense of values. Now what has this to do with the theory of the moral sense or conscience? Is conscience a kind of good taste? Is it a sense of moral values? If so, what are moral values? What does one taste in order to taste morals?

What did Adam and Eve taste when their eyes were opened after the apple incident? They had thought that they ought to share God's knowledge of good and evil, a kind of knowledge essential to human dignity. God had warned them against such an ambition, but was evidently not surprised to learn that the beguiling words of the serpent were more persuasive than his categorical imperative. They had to taste for themselves and find out for themselves. God, being a father, knew the ways of children and realized their urgent need for getting rid of innocence. Once his children's eyes were opened to good and evil, He was, of course, obliged to hold them responsible. They had acted in the hope of learning about good and evil, but received an unexpected lesson in right and wrong. They realized that they were being *held* responsible. In all this affair, there was no question about free will, man's inherent rights, the inherent freedom of consciousness, or any other metaphysical question. There was a conflict of wills and Adam and Eve learned the consequences of such conflicts. They discovered social relations; another will was asserting itself and they were being held accountable for indifference to it. Adam, at first, having had no experience in the field of obligations and no sense of guilt, pretended still to be innocent. To God's straightforward question, he replied evasively, "Eve, she tempted me, and the Serpent tempted her, and God had put the Serpent in the garden." This rational explanation of the event was apparently not what God wanted; and besides, "passing the buck" was charged against him as original sin—and has been anything but original ever since.

Here we have moral tasting in its essence. Others

make us aware of what they expect of us, and if we fail to live up to those expectations, they let us feel that something has gone wrong. Our sensitivity to their attitudes of *holding us responsible* makes us responsive and gradually we become *responsible*. In this way the knowledge of many rights and wrongs, chiefly wrongs, begins to dawn on us; but this knowledge is far from being a knowledge of the principles of right and wrong in general. Specific expectations, claims, obligations are placed upon us, and we learn in the course of practical social relations not to disregard these obligations. We also learn that we are reciprocating, making claims on others and expecting them to be responsive to our acts of holding them responsible. All this moral education is simply an elementary example of animal training, and any psychology text can explain its biological principles. We are animals, complicated and sensitive to be sure, training each other to perform. Our performance and our attitudes toward the process of training measure our responsibility and irresponsibility. If we fail to make progress in this moral art, we may be called morally hopeless and then we may be subjected to a kind of training that is effective on lower animals.

Now, what are the implications of this analysis

for the theory of conscience? First, it implies that if conscience is indeed a form of knowledge, it is a very practical "know-how." It is competence gained from experience in interpersonal relations, knowing how to interpret social reactions, feeling the pull of our social bonds, awareness of the social consequences of conduct. This is the most elementary form of moral knowledge and of good sense. The sense of moral values is an experienced, expert sensitivity and responsiveness toward social expectations and obligations. This training is a training of the emotions. There may be an immediate conformity to and (emotional or habitual) acceptance of the claims made on us, or there may be an emotional rejection of them. Our spontaneous emotional reactions to obligations are apt to be somewhat resentful, since obligations are made for us by others. We react toward them as we would to any other stimulus from our external environment. But our moral judgment or conscience adds to these emotional acceptances or rejections an awareness of how such reactions will be received by those who are holding us responsible. Our consciences bid us not only to evaluate reflectively, instead of emotionally, the claims made on us, but also to consider the emotions and evaluations of our associates. Conscience, far from being mere emotion on the one hand, or disinterested knowledge, on the other, is a two-dimensional judgment and reflects our own tastes as well as our sensitivity to what others expect of us. It is a combination of a sense of values and a sense of responsibility. Both of these so-called senses are really vested interests, the cultivation of which in the context of interpersonal relations constitutes the *art* of morality. In short, morality is a social art, and conscience is a particular kind of social intelligence.

If we take this analysis seriously as an account of the elements of moral experience, we can readily see that our young Buddhist student, mentioned earlier, was mistaken in assuming that one body can have only one conscience. He may have been quite correct in reporting that he could find in himself only a single moral consciousness, for he probably had a relatively integrated social environment. But in the complexities of modern, urban, international life it is quite normal to find persons with a variety of consciences, each concerning some distinct group of social relations. The moral relations within the family, the school, the business, the labor union, the profession, the church, the army, the community, the nation, the United Nations—to mention only a few of the most pervasive types of association which constitute modern society—are far from identical and are seldom integrated thoroughly. Religious communion, secular neighborliness, military discipline, professional obligations are apt to develop distinctive, and even conflicting, consciences, for such groups are organized and have formulated their particular moral codes and ethical principles according to their particular needs and problems. There will be mention in each group of virtues like loyalty, benevolence, generosity, tolerance, but each will give to these virtues a special definition and a varied importance. Consequently, the structure of a normal modern moral consciousness is apt to be pluralistic, relational, more or less disintegrated; and the tensions within a person's normal obligations may well be such as to endanger his personality as an integrated whole. Divided selves are apt to be the result of complicated consciences. Under such practical circumstances the problem of basic principles is apt to be subordinated to the more detailed problems of reconciling diversified systems of responsibilities sufficiently to keep them from undermining personal integrity.

Two types of moral art and ethical theory result from this situation: one is centered in the problem of making the various codes of groups compatible with each other in the context of a single personality; the other is centered on the more general problem of basic principles for any group ethics and hence for morals in general. The former is knowing how to be a responsible member of a variety of associations, each making its own demands; the other is an attempt to discover general norms of responsibility valid for any type of association. Let us look briefly at each type of moral science.

The personal problem is more practical than theoretical; it is less concerned with the nature of conscience, more with how to carry on conscientiously an overload of responsibilities many of which compete with each other either because they are incompatible or because it is physically impossible to do justice to all of them. This problem arises from a commonplace predicament of modern life. It is a temptation to join more associations and cooperative enterprises than one can possibly be an "active" member of. Fortunately there are organizations which do not expect active participation beyond the established monetary dues. But it is precisely the person who takes moral interests most seriously who, out of the most conscientious motives, agrees to responsibilities which prove to be more burdensome than had been anticipated. Thus the extension of

one's moral concerns endangers the conscientiousness with which one pursues any one of them.

There is a school of contemporary British moralists, headed by the late Sir David Ross, which ana-
lyzes such problems as conflicts between *"prima facie
obligations"* and real responsibilities or duties. It is
a *prima facie* obligation to live up to a promise, and
hence it is a *prima facie* obligation not to make more
promises than one can keep. On the other hand, even
a usually conscientious person is apt to create situations of conflict for himself which he did not antici-
pate, perhaps could not have anticipated. Consequently the most common form of moral problem is
to decide which *prima facie* obligations deserve priority. "Priority" has become a convenient escape mech-
anism for the discarding of obligations which do not
enjoy "top priority." The literature of contemporary
business and politics is full of such "priority" talk.
Such talk should be interpreted as a confession that
we have done more promising than we ought to have
done and intend to leave undone what we hope we
can get away with. It is a *prima facie* obligation to
avoid getting into such a predicament. But once in
it (and who is not?), the problem which these British
moral theorists try to solve is to set up a general table
of priorities. The religious person has a ready reply

with his ancient formula: duties to God first, then
to women and children, then to fellow men, lastly
toward one's own self. As an antidote to the natural
tendency to exaggerate what one owes to oneself,
this formula has some merit. But in the majority of
situations such as we have in mind, this formula is
not apt to give a decisive answer. The formulas of
the British moralists are even less helpful. I refer
you to them, but I blush to repeat them here. For it
seems to me that there is something radically wrong
in the theory that it is *rational* to be able to set up
a table such that ideally a computing machine could
solve our moral problems for us. Jeremy Bentham
had this idea long ago, and, though the Utilitarians
have for the most part abandoned it, the idea keeps
reappearing in unexpected places. One basic fallacy
here lies in the idea of absolute priority. This term
implies that rational preference involves setting up
the rival alternatives in an order of preferability or
scale of obligatoriness. The supposition is that there
is a property called in Germany "worthiness," in
England "admirability," in India "purity" or
"truthfulness," and in feudal cultures "nobility,"
which can serve as the measure or criterion for put-
ting the incompatibles in their proper places. If one
such criterion is insufficient in some cases, a few

others can be added, which complicates the calcu-
lation but does not change the theory in general.

In fact, however, moral decisions, whether reasonable or unreasonable, are not arrived at in this way.
No general "abilities" are decisive in a concrete situation. Which of a number of alternative obligations is *the* duty to be performed in this situation
is and should be determined on the spot (not in
advance) in view of the particular importance of
the competing obligations in this particular array
of circumstances, not in view of a general, fixed list
of priorities. Priorities vary with circumstances. The
most rational decision is the most appropriate response to the situation, and this propriety cannot
be calculated either in advance or by fixed norms.
The prime responsibility is to be responsive to the
actual demands of the real situation. These must
each be felt and appreciated in terms of "Who expects what of me now?" And then from the co-
presence of these various responsibilities in their
concrete meanings for the interests at stake, there
emerges a conviction that *"this one* is the *right* action here and now." Such judgment of "right-here-
and-now" makes useless the listing in order of the
rejected "wrongs." Rightness usually appears under
the guise of "probably-the-least-troublemaking" of

the possible acts at the time. If, as in a game of chess, all the possible moves could be listed and all the rules were fixed and the number of possible situations were finite, it would be possible to refer "the-right-move-in-this-situation" to a computer. But so long as life is not a closed game, so long must conscientious action involve a practical moral art: skill, experience, insight, imagination, cleverness, originality are all of them factors in right judgment. The best reason can do is to discipline each of these factors for what it is worth; reason can never answer such problems independently of art, nor conscience independently of experience. Responsibility is achieved as it is in all the arts by learning the various skills required. The road to acting responsibly is by learning the hard way. Short cuts to moral knowledge are perilous.

The impersonal problem of ethical theory, the problem of general principles, has, I hope, been clarified by what has been said about the personal problem of responsibility. If we try to differentiate between the right and the good as categories; in other words, if we distinguish moral deliberation from evaluation in general, there are a few general propositions about right conduct which follow from the preceding considerations.

1. The right action is the appropriate action. Propriety is by its nature determined concretely. There are various proprieties in varying times and places. Propriety can be defined abstractly, but there is no concrete knowledge of propriety in general, any more than there is of goodness in general.

2. Moral rightness or propriety involves what might be called public decency. Propriety is determined by what those various groups or publics expect of their members which have a vested interest in a given situation. These expectations should be as definite and publicly known as possible, for it is on the basis of this whole complex of demands upon him that the moral agent must act.

3. A person's conscience is compounded of the various responsibilities to which he is held by his associations, past, present, and ideal. For the groups which have a hold on consciences are by no means all contemporary, nor are they all content to regard propriety in terms of traditional decencies. Idealized decencies also enter into the total situation of an enlightened conscience. But such ideals are not created by the individual's conscience alone; they enter his conscience as actual demands of the ideals of an actual group of which he is a responsive and responsi-

ble member. In other words, interpersonal relations involve conflicts of ideals when the ideals are actually held by groups, for a group's ideals are an intrinsic element in its interests and attitudes. Ideals impose a kind of *ought* on us by their very nature as ideals; but they impose an additional, moral ought on us when they are the ideals held by those who hold us responsible for a regard for their ideals.

4. Conscientiousness requires much more than "good will" whether this term be taken in the sense of "meaning well" or in the Kantian sense of "willing the universal" *(volonté générale).* It is not a mere knowledge of the right in general, nor a loyalty to the commonweal, nor a benevolent spirit. Nor is it moral freedom. It is a type of social bondage. Conscientiousness is (a) sensitivity to the burden of obligation which each social situation imposes on an agent, plus (b) good taste in judging proprieties, plus (c) a critical sense of the values at stake. Being merely a conscientious performer of obligations without a pursuit of happiness would define an inhuman moral monster. A good, human sense of responsibility must be supplemented by a right judgment of values; and ethics is no decent science unless it is in partnership with good taste in other matters.

# II

## RELIGIOUS
## EXPERIENCE
## AND
## SECULAR
## ETHICS

I T is not my purpose here to explain how a secular morality is possible. The actual existence of secular morals and of purely secular systems of ethical doctrine seems to me to make it a futile academic gesture to insist, as some moralists still do, that religion is a necessary foundation for morals. If I had the gifts of an Immanuel Kant, I might ask: How are these secular moralities possible? And I would try to answer such a question. But I am content to let the facts of secular morality speak for themselves, and to take for granted that whatever is actual must have been possible.

Nor am I concerned with the question: Which type of ethics is better, religious or secular? Such a general value judgment would be difficult to arrive at, and probably of little use when arrived at, since both religious and secular morals vary enormously from very good to horrible. I am not judging here; I am trying to answer a purely factual question: What difference does religion make to ethics? But I am not taking religions and morals in all their diversity; this would be a monumental task. I shall venture a schematic answer, taking a fairly common conception of what it means to be religious, and a fairly common conception of what it means to be moral. I shall speak not of religions and moralities as social institutions and historical entities, but of two types of experiences, or better, of two aspects of experience, the religious and the moral. This is evidently a simplification of the problem—intentionally so. But I hope my schematic treatment may be suggestive for more empirical, more anthropological and sociological studies.

My chief aim here in using a dimensional metaphor to distinguish religious and secular morals is to show how figurative and meaningful, how suggestive and imaginative our most common terms are. Our most ordinary language for moral experience provides us with a moral map which makes self-orientation much better and simpler than do the more learned languages of scientific ethics. It provides us with what mathematicians in their technical language would call a practical vector analysis.

I shall represent the common language of secular morality as suggesting moral movement on a horizontal axis, and the religious language as suggesting movement along a vertical axis. My justification is, as you will see, that the languages themselves suggest such a scheme. I shall examine the language of moving forward and backward; then the language of moving up and down; then analyze the results of their interaction.

The concept of making progress seems to be clearly secular. Let us examine what it means to go *forward*. If a soldier hears, "Forward march!" he knows in what direction to go. "Forward" means definitely "ahead" or "as you face." But then suddenly he hears another command, "To the rear, march!" and he knows exactly what to do. He must turn in the opposite direction. Then, after marching a little in that direction, he hears again, "To the rear," and he knows that what used to be forward is now to the rear. It is best not to have a sense of direction at all on the drill field; merely follow "directions." In any case, a philosophical recruit would be obliged to conclude from his experience on the drill field that "forward" does not mean any particular direction. But under battle conditions, he soon learns that this is not true; "forward" is into the face of the enemy, and "to the rear" means retreat. In either case, whether on the drill field or in battle, the army does not use these terms ambiguously or metaphorically. But here we are, neither on the drill field nor in battle, and if someone were to ask, as I am now asking, "Are you going forward or backward?" you would know at once that a sermon is to follow. Each one would be supposed to start a moral self-analysis and to ask himself, "How am I doing?" This is metaphor. The spatial terms of direction are now not being interpreted literally in terms of locomotion, but vaguely in terms of something conceived as "moral movement." You imagine that your moral movement has direction, forwards or backwards, but when you stop to think you really do not know what either direction means. You might try to explain your going forward by saying that you are going in the direction you are facing. But now you are using "facing" metaphorically. You may be told by a philosopher that you are facing the future; and if you believe him, you are committed to the comforting insight that you are inevitably going forward all the time, for temporally there is no other place to go except into the future. So, "forward" cannot mean "into the future," unless you are willing to believe that progress is inevitable. Now, if I ask, not *"Where* are you facing?" but *"What* are you facing?" you may get another metaphorical idea. "What I really face," you reply, "is my work, my job, my responsibilities. That's what is always ahead of me, wherever I turn." But this answer won't do, even though it uses concepts of moral experience literally; for while at work, on the job, you sometimes think, "I'm getting ahead," and at other times you admit, "This is getting me nowhere." Now where is "ahead" and where is "nowhere"? Do you really have a sense of direction in this matter? Where did you expect to go? Are you "on the go" at all? What do you mean by *moving* morally? Is forward perhaps the direction of hope or of imagined happiness? Possibly. But probably you have not thought that far "ahead." In any case, where do you suppose "happiness" lies? If I keep insisting with my, "Which way is forward?" you may well get impatient and say, in retreat, "Well, anyway, I try to go the straight and narrow path." Here again are the spatial metaphors. But here the trouble is that most narrow paths are not straight. Are you going ahead in a straight line, or are you tacking, zigzag? My father used to preach to us:

> Oh, it's not the gale, but the set of the sail
> That determines the way we go.

This sounds true enough, but it is again metaphorical truth. How do I know whether I am tacking or sailing with the wind? Tacking is more trouble, to be sure. Perhaps our sense of effort indicates the right direction? "Going with the tide is drifting," we say. "Upstream" is "ahead"! But when the effort seems futile, then what? Simply more effort? Or change of direction?

Our spatial metaphors seem to be driving us around in circles. Suppose we give up trying to decide which way is "forward." Suppose we take the negative way and say, "I may not know when I'm going ahead, but I know I'm not standing still, and I know very well when I'm taking a step backwards." A sense of failure is more keen than a sense of success, and may be a more reliable moral signpost. This seems to be good common sense, though it is still expressed in the spatial metaphors. Let us ac-

cept this as a fairly definite point of moral orientation. After all, I want to get "ahead" with the argument, and not quibble. Admitting then that a sense
of failure is relatively definite and that we can usually tell which way is backward, let us suppose that
when we find ourselves going backwards, if we turn
"to the rear" (which, of course, is a metaphorical
rear in this case) we shall be going forward. Not
having to face discouragement step by step is in itself an encouragement. We may then conclude that
so long as we are not being continually discouraged,
we may be going ahead. We can assume that we are
then going right even if we have no idea where this
direction is leading. In other words, it would seem
that progress is not so much a direction as a way of
going, a kind of stepping. *Where* we are going seems
quite indefinite, but "the going is good."

Now let us look at what we have learned metaphorically. Let us represent the line of success and
failure by a horizontal arrow pointing to the right.
Going right will represent moral motion in the direction of progress and going left will represent ret-
rogression. (Here "right" and "left" are *not* taken
metaphorically.) The road ahead, to the right,
points we know not where, but as far as it goes the
going is good. We know we are "on our way" even

though we don't know *where* we are going. This is a matter of step-by-step. The right end of the arrow, then, we must label "step-by-step good going," and at the head of the arrow we can put only a question mark.

On the left end of the arrow, backwards, we can put "failure," for there the road seems to end, and along the road in that direction there is step-by-step discouragement. Failure is a state of collapse that results from one misstep after another. Whereas success is not so much a goal at the end of the road as a cumulating confidence along the way. The Greeks had a saying, "Never count a man happy until you know his end." And we repeat the old proverb, with Shakespeare, "All's well that ends well." This puts too much emphasis on the end of the road, it seems to me, and is more true of the left end of the way than the right. But it implies the truth that one can never be sure of progress until one quits moving, and then, like the Last Judgment, the knowledge comes too late. But going backwards, we occasionally come to a dead end, when we are "up against a stone wall," and when there is nothing to do but go into reverse or quit. In short, going forwards and backwards is really not a matter of direction at all, but of kinds of experience. Nevertheless, the directional metaphors of our everyday speech help us to measure and express something that is really very complicated. Let this pass for a common sense, elementary analysis of moral life along the horizontal secular axis of action or movement. This is the *practical* dimension of moral experience, and reflects the moral values and disvalues of ordinary daily work and conduct.

But there is another dimension, governed by another set of spatial metaphors—the up and down axis. I shall represent this dimension, accordingly, by a vertical axis cutting at right angles the axis of action. What do "up" and "down" mean morally? Going up and down is not a matter of taking steps as is movement along the practical axis; the vertical axis is an axis of mood and imagination, an axis of motive rather than of motion. When we are cast down emotionally, we feel "let down" or "down and out." When we look up for help, we look up as far as we can see and farther; there is no sense in looking up a step at a time. We try to reach all the way to the top. "On high" is our source of strength. The Heavenly Father is "up there"—not in the sky, of course, for there is no physical up and down. We say that we are dependent on our "superiors," those "above" us. Authority, inspiration, revelation—all are said to come from above. We are clearly dealing with metaphors here, and with the most common metaphors of religious language. "Up" is spiritually up, upright, on a higher level. But how can one measure the various "heights" of these so-called levels? This vertical axis reaching to heaven above and to "the abyss" below, I might call the axis of aspiration and desperation. Our visions of blessedness carry us much higher than we can hope to go, and our fears let us down with a dreadful feeling of falling, from which we usually "bounce back." Our ups and downs along this axis have greater range and less duration than our steps along the horizontal axis. We have our moments of uplift, elevation, exaltation, high spirits; then the other extreme of descent, dejections, down in the dumps, or the depths of despair. Our emotional and spiritual barometer rises and falls quickly and often drastically.

In short, moral experience is of a very different character along the two axes: there is a plodding, slow, step-by-step advance or retreat horizontally, and there is the rapid fluctuating, moody change of motivation vertically.

These two axes are not by nature correlated; they vary independently. We shall not inquire into origins here, nor undertake a less metaphorical analysis. Our common, spatial metaphors are excellent for suggesting two contrasting dimensions of moral experience. The one is practical, problematical, experimental, groping, striving, meeting obligations and opportunities along the way, taking them in stride; it involves the social world of interpersonal conduct, agreements and disagreements, trials and errors, successes and failures. It is the secular life of daily affairs. Using another metaphor, we call it our outer, extravert, external experience. The other dimension is our inner life, more private, intimate, reflective, introspective—introverted emoting and imagining, our ups and downs. This aspect of experience can have a purely secular expression, but the richer and fuller it is, the more its expression is apt to approach the religious forms. "Spirituality" is not necessarily religious, but is commonly so taken. There is extravert religion and there are introvert forms of secular interests. But on the whole we are justified in associating the dimension of progress with secular experience, and the dimension of uplift-and-dejection with religious experience. Admitting, then, that this is not a strictly accurate correlation, it seems significant enough to associate our dominant secular concerns with the horizontal axis and our dominant religious concerns with the vertical axis. We may then see clearly that secular morals and religious morals are independent variables. They are qualitatively distinct, and they represent different aspects of experience. But no experience is apt to be exclusively of one or the other type; both dimensions are usually represented. Their various effects on each other create the chief problems and situations of moral experience. We seldom find ourselves directly on one or the other of these axes. Life is lived off-center, somewhere in one or the other of the four quadrants formed by the axes. Let us look in turn at the moral life in each of these quadrants.

In the Northeast quadrant the two axes reinforce each other. As we *move* forward and *are carried* upward, we find ourselves in a diagonal position, along the component of forces, going uphill, or rather up steps. The gain in altitude gives us a vantage point. We can see the road ahead better and gain perspective. And in spite of the uphill work we gain momentum; encouragement is emotional as well as practical. Our religious imaginations and attitudes, too, change character as we move them forwards, inclining them toward our practical interests. Our dreams and visions take on a more practical quality and become working ideals or faiths; they enable us to draw idealized models for our practical affairs. We seem to see further. Our work becomes more interesting and our obligations less burdensome. Our progress in action has a "lift" to it and raises our whole existence to a higher plane. The rise is not apt to be steady, but the net movement is along the diagonal upward. Our vertical moods and tempers are apt to carry us up and down by fits and jumps. But the net effect of this zigzagging up and down, instead of sticking to the level road, is to make the moral life more exciting than it could ever be if we lived only on the flat plains of practical progress. And as we look up the slope toward the far Northeast, we catch occasional glimpses of the Platonic heaven of pure ideals and perfect bliss. Heaven comes somewhat down to earth.

In the Southeast quadrant, life looks quite different. We go forward, but the road turns into ruts. We keep on going right, but joylessly; there seems to be nothing ahead but more labor and fatigue. In one sense the work, being downhill, is easier; it becomes a routine, simple and dull. But as we keep going lower, getting further from the heavenly heights, we become sceptical. Is it worth the effort? What has practical success to do with genuine satisfaction? Wouldn't we be better off if we forgot about progress and indulged our dreams and desires? There should be a ladder straight up to heaven, with angels escorting us up and down, instead of this dreary fallen estate into which Adam and Eve plunged us. But the ladder is imaginary, so we keep on our virtuous, plodding way. This quadrant corresponds very roughly to the region which Dante, in his classic moral geography, portrayed as the region of whirling banners. Here wills are vacillating, the sense of direction is lost, doubt and confusion haunt the toilers amid their many temptations. Life here is full of temptations and morale is always on trial. Discipline for discipline's sake! What an inhuman, profitless existence! And yet life goes forward on and on, at best in boredom, at worst sullenly, blindly, downhill. There is thus a tendency for the imagination to turn not vertically up and down, but diagonally Southeast toward *nausea,* and backward toward the Northwest, as if in fits of nostalgia.

So, let us examine this Northwest quadrant next. Here men look up for hope and drop down for opiates. The world of illusions is so much more attractive than the actual world of practical morals. Let us flee the world, they say, and contemplate heaven; let us lock ourselves in monasteries or deserts and live in solitude or cloisters. Here there is security and peace. There are golden ages to look back towards. Backwards lie the good old days. True advance is to turn the back on the world, so that it may not distract our vision from the view of a better world. Be detached! Cling to nothing on earth, for you can't drag it upward; it will drag you down. Rise up in spirit into the realm where the spirit is free from the cares and wants of existence. It is only in contemplation that man finds rest. Pull up anchor and sail out under the stars; be guided by them alone and dismiss the beacons of shores and ports, for out on the deep man naturally looks upward. Drifting under heaven is better than slaving on land. With such slogans and metaphors men cut themselves loose from their horizontal moorings and allow themselves to be carried backwards and upwards. This is the region of space ships, the flight against gravity, moral skyrocketing. It is an ancient disease and still contagious. Up, up, higher until the earth appears as small as it really is in celestial perspective. "Dust thou art, to dust returneth, was not spoken of the soul," hence this dusty life on earth is not real, not earnest. There is something fascinating about this transcendental freedom, beyond good and evil, nearer to union with the Alone.

Such soaring philosophy has found its best expressions among the mystics, most of whom left behind them an early career of frustration and failure. I have no doubt that the world is richer for harboring such mystics, but the fact remains that in secular perspective they are moral parasites. Their irresponsible upward flights are at the expense of practical reason, and if men generally followed them, there would soon be no more physical fuel for the flights. *Some* souls must remain on earth, their moral feet resting on terra firma. *Some* there must always be who can distinguish genuine illusions from the supposed unreality of the solid world. The world may be too much with us, but without it we soon lose our bearings completely.

This popular metaphor of "upwards" is exceptionally beguiling; men easily imagine that there is a way "straight up," talking and thinking as if there were a physical rising above the physical earth. The power of this elevating metaphor creates some of the most serious problems of the moral life, for such flights, when they return to earth, land far behind the starting point. The faith in "the suspension of the ethical," to use Kierkegaard's phrase for this radically religious life, has led to the downfall of many a would-be pilgrim, dragging him down out of his vain flight into the Northeast toward *Utopia* and other exalted regions of non-being.

The fall down from the Northwestern quadrant takes us into the Southwestern quadrant. This is Dante's hell: "All hope abandon ye who enter here." Reliance on opiates of the people, whether religious or secular, creates the illusion that all is illusion. It creates an artificial world of illusory satisfactions which bring tortures in their trail. The most fatal of these illusions is the belief that the moral world has no upward dimension at all, and since hope springs from the upward look more than from the forward march, this illusion kills hope. And with hope gone, there remains only the tragic charity that damned souls may feel for each other. There is society of a sort in hell, for sympathy is most conspicuous among those who need it most. The road down the Southwest decline is not a lonely road, nor is it without its gaieties. Hopelessness has its own ways of celebrating. Only, these poor Southwestern souls have no illusions about going either up or forward. They face back and down consciously, like explorers of the deep. They may even be moral philosophers like Dante, whose wonderful exploration of the realm of punishments has always been the most interesting and instructive part of his *Divine Comedy*. It is possible to endure hell and hopelessness, but it is an endurance test which has no point except to a philosopher who has lost all interests save the interest in the knowledge gained by eating the fruits on the tree of evil—a Eugene O'Neill kind of mind and imagination, which has a subhuman sympathy for the down-and-out.

This completes our survey of the two dimensions of morality and of the metaphors of forward-backward and up-down. The picture it gives us of the varieties of moral experience seems to me to afford a simple scheme for orientation. It suggests a few conclusions which have some importance as hypotheses for a more technical and adequate analysis:

1. Religious and secular morality have independent developments.

2. Religion and morality may support or obstruct each other.

3. The inner dimension of the moral life is expressed and enriched by religious metaphors, symbols, and imaginative constructs.

4. The double perspective of the two axes is necessary for an adequate interpretation of morality.

5. Secular morality has a steadying influence on religious experience, and religious experience adds significance and energy to secular moral intelligence and effort.

6. The opposition in Spinoza's philosophy between the ethics of bondage (social, secular) and the ethics of freedom (intellectual love of God) needs to be supplemented by an analysis which shows how the two may reinforce each other.

The basic point, however, which this description of the two kinds of ethics is intended to make clear is that the normal relation between them is not an either/or relation, as if a person had to choose one of them, but rather it is a relation of interpenetration. Neither would be complete without the other and neither is foundation for the other. They affect each other by giving life four possible directions or patterns, each of which is symptomatic of a distinct type of character. And none of these types would be significant without the double perspective.

There is, however, a type of religious experience which claims to go "beyond" or "above" moral experience, and which Walter Lippmann has significantly called "high religion."

A mature desire is innocent. This, I think, is the final teaching of the great sages. "To him who has finished the Path, and passed beyond sorrow, who has freed himself on all sides, and thrown away every fetter, there is no more fever of grief," says a Buddhist writer.

"The Master said,
At fifteen I had my mind bent on learning,
At thirty, I stood firm.
At forty, I had no doubts,
At fifty, I knew the decrees of Heaven,
At sixty, my ear was an obedient organ for the reception of truth,
At seventy, I could follow what my heart desired, without transgressing what was right."

To be able, as Confucius here indicates, to follow what the heart desires without coming into collision with the stubborn facts of life is the privilege of the utterly innocent and of the utterly wise. It is the privilege of the infant and of the sage who stand at the two poles of experience; of the infant because the world ministers to his heart's desire and of the sage because he has learned what to desire. Perhaps this is what Jesus meant when he told his followers that they must become like little children.

If this is what he meant, and if this is what Buddha, Confucius, and Spinoza meant, then we have here the clue to the function of high religion in human affairs. I venture, at least, to suggest that the function of high religion is to reveal to men the quality of mature experience, that high religion is a prophecy and an anticipation of what life is like when desire is in perfect harmony with reality. It announces the discovery that men can enter into the realm of the spirit when they have outgrown all childishness. *(A Preface to Morals* [New York, 1929], pp. 192-193.)

This theory, that a religious life can carry a person into a mature second childhood or innocence, leaving morality behind and below, is very attractive, especially to those who are approaching old age and are wearied by moral experience. But neither this theory nor this religious practice is quite as innocent as it imagines itself, and it may become mature to the point of rottenness. There have been sages who have demonstrated that this ideal is attainable, but for one sage there are hundreds of those whom this ambition has reduced to childishness. After long years of "maturity" a person is quite naturally tempted to believe he has attained innocence. But the mortification of the flesh, the cessation of desire, the love of rest, create their own moral problems and dangers. And the chief danger is this confusion between genuine innocence and jaded maturity. There is no return from experience to innocence, as there is no way to unlearn what has been learned or to undo what has been done. It takes further experience and distinctive disciplines to make amends for errors; it takes a discipline of forgetting and forgiving to erase the past; and it takes positive virtues to find absolute rest in God. This is no mere innocence and no ascension above morality; it is a culmination of the cooperation of religion and morals; it may be both at their best. But when these heights have been attained, the extreme altitude may well cause loss of perspective and acute dizziness. It takes "sageliness," as the Chinese say, to maintain this exalted equilibrium, for no man ascends directly into highest heaven where morality, progress, work, and cares, life itself are submerged in the eternal praises and heavenly music of the innocent angels.

# III
## MANKIND
## AND
## MORALS

MANY years ago, during World War I, while I was still an active student, a classmate of mine in the course of a discussion on group ethics asked the professor what seemed to the rest of us in the class a foolish question, and I imagine he, too, asked it merely to tease the teacher. He pretended to want to know if it would be possible for the whole of mankind to function as a single group. Could all men ever get together in such a way that they might be said to be a moral community? We had been discussing family morals, tribal morals, gang morals, boy scout morals, chamber of commerce morals, Christian morals, national morals, international morals, class-conflict morals, club morals, fraternity morals, professional ethics, business ethics—would it make any sense in this context to speak of human morals or of an ethics for humanity? Obviously not, thought the rest of us; mankind may be a species but it is not a community, and where there is no community, how can there be a moral order? To our amazement, our patient, speculative old professor took the question seriously. There might be a situation which could be called "a human situation" in the practical sense, in which a common effort might make all men actively cooperative. The earth might find itself some day involved in a conflict with Mars! Lacking some such interglobal conflict, the professor admitted, it would be difficult to imagine how all men could be comrades, teammates, pulling together as if they belonged together. World-wide morality would have to be a world-wide fighting *morale*. Something like an interglobal war would be needed to give any genuine meaning to the trite phrase of human brotherhood. Where there is no common cause, there are no common obligations. After all, morality is an obligation, not a luxury, and no one would take the trouble to preach loyalty when it was not needed. Men do not tie themselves up in moral knots unless there is some common good to be achieved. Give men a common enemy and they generate spontaneously a common morale. Give men universal peace and mankind inevitably disintegates. Some such thesis was the general presupposition on which our course in practical group ethics was based. Without a world-wide mission it would be foolish to think of world-wide morals. To us, and even to the more imaginative professor, the possibility of finding any practical motive for a universal human cooperative spirit seemed so remote that we took for granted that our academic speculations were utopian and somewhat comic.

But within the short span of a single generation, this utopian comedy has become a tragic reality. All mankind is today huddled together in a common fear. The purely speculative "state of nature" about which Thomas Hobbes wrote so eloquently, and which historians assured us was a purely speculative creation, has suddenly loomed up before all mankind as an overwhelming, immediate menace. The "war of all against all" could instantly make human life "solitary, poor, nasty, brutish and short." In such a state there would be "no place for industry; no commodious building; no instruments of moving, and removing such things as require much force; no knowledge of the face of the earth; no account of time; no arts; no letters; no society." *(Leviathan,* part 1, Chap. 13.)

Being thus united for a few years by a universal fear, mankind has already laid a tangible though negative basis for a universal human morality. It is not true, despite what we have been taught recently, that "we have nothing to fear but fear." Thank God for fear! For one danger which it creates, there are a hundred dangers from which it saves us. There are times when men ought to be fearful. Mankind's common fear has now generated a common concern; the common concern has generated a common publicity; the publicity has generated communication; the communication has stimulated curiosity; the curiosity has led to inquiry; and symptoms of a genuine human sympathy of all for all are beginning to show above the ground level of global fear; a morality for mankind seems to be in the making.

The "human situation" is already something more than an ultimate concern for an imminent end of the world. We are no longer sharing the excitements of the prophets of Doomsday. Henry Adams,

who in the early years of the century calculated that
by mid-century "radiant energy" would become explosive and blow the whole human world to bits,
and the other gloomy visionaries of his day, now
lie peacefully buried with their books. Though the
danger still looms, more positive concerns and more
hopeful possibilities are already gathering momentum. From the physics of Henry Adams men are
turning increasingly to the pacifics of Jane Addams.
As early as 1922, in her book *Peace and Bread in
Time of War,* which has fortunately been repub-
lished (1945), Jane Addams, speaking from long
years of practical experience, called attention to the
futility of building a moral order for mankind on
the foundation of politics, police, and coercion.
These more official forms of power find their useful-
ness only after a context of moral strength and a
practical cooperative power make them tolerable
and tolerated. To begin the creation of the community of mankind by trying to establish world government, in the hope that this global state would then
provide bread, work, and music for all, is to begin
at the wrong end. The foundations must be laid before the roof, and the digging deep comes before the
foundations can be laid well. Building community
is an art as well as an obligation. To begin with

pure obligation is building castles in the thin air
of promises. Here Hobbes has misled us: the social
contract is the culmination not the foundation of
community. Any businessman knows that contracts
are essential to good business, but he knows also that
no one will sign a contract with a firm that is not
already well in business. Constructive work must
precede collective coercion. The implication of such
business sense for moral theory has been put well
by John Dewey, when he commented as follows on
Jane Addams' book:

> Miss Addams repeatedly called attention to the fact
> that all social movements *outside* of traditional diplo-
> macy and "international law" had been drawing the
> peoples of different countries together in even closer
> bonds, while war, under present conditions, was affect-
> ing civilian populations as it had never done before.
> Both of these factors have immensely increased since
> she wrote. The futility of dependence upon old meth-
> ods . . . has correspondingly increased.
>
> In contrast, the process of organization upon which
> Miss Addams would have us depend is one which cuts
> *across* nationalistic lines. Moreover, instead of setting
> up a super-state, it also cuts *under* these lines. . . .
> [There is] a recognition of the "Food Challenge" for
> world organization. The energy with which we use
> and extend this kind of process as the working model

for other endeavors at international organization will decide the success or failure of efforts to achieve lasting peace. This is no mere prediction, but is based on the solid experience of the past. ("The Realism of Jane Addams," introduction to *Peace and Bread in Time of War* [New York, 1945], pp. xiii-xix, *passim*.)

There is no reason why a global government is necessary to distribute food world-wide, to promote health and basic education, or to bring the joys of music and the lesser arts to all mankind. World-wide trade and world-wide religious missions were established before there was any world-wide politics or international law. In general, whether a community be local or world-wide, it must have grass roots before it can have good government. The moral structure of a community grows from the ground *up* and not *down* from the authorities on top.

Taking this as a general analysis of mankind's present situation, and before going into the practical problem of how a world-wide moral structure may be cultivated internationally and transnationally, we ought to consider how to conceive the general theory or science of such a structure. How can we formulate an ethics or a method of moral science which would serve the cause of morals for all mankind? There are two traditional answers to this problem which deserve our attention and criticism. The one theory rests on faith in a universal moral order and its so-called "law of nature." There are supposed to be universal moral principles which can be discovered and formulated. The other theory rests on faith in a universal scale of values. One theory asserts that all men are subject to universal moral rules or principles; the other that all men have common, ultimate values or goals. According to one, morality has a universal rational foundation; according to the other, it has a universal purpose or good. One relies on the logic of law, the other on the philosophy of values. Let us examine each.

I shall not recall to you the ancient origins and long career of natural law theory. The most eminent writers on jurisprudence have subscribed to it—Confucius, Cicero, St. Thomas, Hobbes, Grotius, Leibniz, Blackstone, Adam Smith, Immanuel Kant, Thomas Jefferson—to mention a few of them. What concerns us more than this respectable history of the doctrine is the fact that natural law theory is being revived today by both moralists and jurists. There seems to be a persistent faith in this doctrine which inclines many to believe that there must be an eternal need for it. Is it dictated by human nature, by reason, or by experience? Whichever of these three traditionally assigned grounds is given for it, natural law is believed to be authoritative for all human beings always. It is therefore no accident that today, when all mankind needs moral unification, there should be a new and vigorous appeal to a law of nature to which all men are subject because it has absolute authority.

Note these contemporary American reassertions of natural law:

> This law conforms to the essence of human nature which He [God] has created. It is that aspect of the eternal law which directs the actions of men. . . . Natural law is discoverable by reason alone. Natural law has been promulgated in the intellect. At least as regards its more fundamental principles it is knowable proximately through the conscience.
>
> The most basic ideal of this law, namely, that every man must live in accordance with his rational nature, so that he will do good and avoid evil, is self-evident to all. (Brenden F. Brown, "The Natural Law, the Marriage Bond, and Divorce," *Fordham Law Review*, XXIV [1955], 83.)
>
> Natural law, by conforming to the dispassionate process of intellectual argument, claims truth for the judicious assertion that the world as a whole no less than our total legal experience furnishes actual support for the significance of values and objective standards.

In this, natural law contributes decisively to the trans-
lation of mere hopes or dreams into the actual realization of what is good, true, and just. It is also declaratory
of an eminently decent and intelligent attitude which
continuously asserts that the standards of right and
wrong, good and evil are real and as such are truly
effective in the lives of men. (Anton-Hermann C.
Chroust, "Natural Law and Legal Positivism," *Ohio
State Law Journal,* XIII [1952], 179.)

Men at all times and places find it necessary to
appeal from the inadequacies of actual norms or
positive law to an ideal conceived as a "higher law."
Here the word "higher" means in practice "more
binding," "more authoritative." And this need is
felt not only by those who feel injured by actual
norms, but also by judges who must have some sanction to give authority to their particular verdicts in-
terpreting what the law says. It is true, as a matter
of fact, that it is usually possible, in any given case,
to appeal beyond the positive law to some recognized
norm that is more general and more reasonable. But
it is a too common tendency among men who wish to
be reasonable to think of this higher law as also absolute, binding always, everywhere. It is a far cry from
practical appeals toward a "higher up" to a universal
code that is evidently and eternally valid, enthroned

in the Highest or in the court of pure reason. For
critics have been able to show that whenever a specific content is given to "justice," "righteousness,"
"the Will of God," or "pure reason," some local conviction or fallible conscience always creeps in for
sanctification and hopes to be endowed with the halo
of absolute truth, which it does not merit. Paul
Vinogradoff explains admirably what it is that actually happens when men appeal to the universal
natural law:

> It is an appeal by society at large, or by the best
> spirits of a given society, not against single decisions
> or rules, but against entire systems of positive law.
> Legislators are called in to amend law by separate stat-
> utes; judges may do a good deal in amending the law
> by decisions in individual cases, but the wisdom of
> legislators and the equity of judges are by themselves
> powerless against systems, because they start from the
> recognition of the authority of positive law in general.
> And yet law, being a human institution, ages not only
> in its single rules and doctrines, but in its national and
> historical setting, and the call for purification and re-
> form may become more and more pressing with every
> generation. Public opinion, then, turns from reality to
> ideals. Speculation arises as to the essentials of law as
> conceived in the light of justice. Of course these con-
> ceptions of justice are themselves historical, but they

are drawn not from the complicated compromises of
positive law but from the simpler and more scientific
teaching of philosophical doctrine. Thus the contents
of the law of nature vary with the ages, but their aim is
constant; it is justice. (*Common Sense in Law* [New
York, 1915], pp. 244-245.)

The only question I would raise here is Vinogradoff's reference to "the simpler and more scientific teaching of philosophical doctrines." It may be
that from a lawyer's perspective philosophy seems
relatively "simple" and "scientific," but he would
get few philosophers to agree with him. Having
struggled with the writings of philosophers most of
my life, I must confess that I have not found them to
be either simple or scientific. A philosopher is a good
example of a person who feels an extraordinary need
for universality and rationality. These ideals are his
professional aims; as they are also the aims of a professional judge. But a philosopher always falls far
short of his aim, as any other philosopher will testify.
Mr. Justice Oliver Wendell Holmes, after reading
John Dewey's *Experience and Nature,* wrote to a
friend, "So me-thought God would have spoken had
He been inarticulate but keenly desirous to tell you
how it was." (*Holmes-Pollock Letters,* II [Cam-
bridge, 1941], 287.) This is the impression any phi-

losopher hopes to make on any reader. But philosophers are nevertheless human and their ambitions to speak even inarticulately the Word of God are in vain.

In short, admitting that the appeal to a higher law is a common need among men, men have to date been unable to formulate the contents of natural law with sufficient generality and authority to make their formulations useful bases for a universal ethics. The cultural diversities in mankind run deep, and successfully thwart any attempts to make a universal portrait of man's inherent dignity and decency or to promulgate maxims of justice which would be respected as rational in any culture. It would not be enough to prove that there has been always everywhere a morality of some kind or other. All men may have consciences, but what is demanded by the faith in natural law is that all men at bottom should have the same conscience; and that is expecting too much either of human nature or of human civilization.

Turning now to the second approach to our theoretical problem, the belief that there is a universal set of values or goals which all men have in common, I shall begin by presenting a recent formulation of this idea by a philosopher in India. He writes:

The question whether there can be a hierarchy of

values common to all cultures needs to start with the idea that man in both the hemispheres belongs to the same species and must have some common basic values on which different cultural patterns have been built up. . . . Any culture is determined by values which are common to all cultures and also by those which are peculiar to itself. . . . As the basic nature of man is the same everywhere, there must necessarily be a set of basic values common to man everywhere. He may be unconscious of them so long as he is ignorant; he may support some differences as decisive because of historical reasons which create vested interests; or he may overemphasize differences for political purposes. But given the ability and the freedom to think and the good will to appreciate, he will see that man and his values are essentially the same everywhere. . . . When man in undeveloped countries and cultures is educated, he also wants to be free. . . . There is a simple argument to show that man has to be assumed to be the same everywhere. Psychology, biology, physiology, anatomy, social philosophy, ethics, religion, metaphysics are all meant to be common to all people. There may be different systems; but no philosopher or scientist thinks that his philosophy or science is meant for a particular culture. . . . We have to assume, therefore, that not only the basic nature of man but also the values he lives for and ought to enjoy must be the same, whatever be the religion or culture to which he belongs. . . . Not only should every man treat every other man of his culture as he wishes to be treated by him; but also every nation

should treat every other nation as it wishes to be
treated by the latter. . . . Even after accepting the situa-
tional view of values and saying that in any given situation the individual may be allowed free choice between
equally important alternatives, can we still grade values
in a general way as higher and lower? . . . In a true
hierarchy, just as the lower is controlled by the higher,
the higher should depend on the lower for realization.
. . . A more detailed conception of hierarchy may be
given by basing it on the Indian conception of man.
. . . The three so-called spiritual values and the su-
preme spiritual value of God-realization give rise to the
problem of the value of freedom. The three activities—
intellectual, ethical and aesthetic—result in the inward
transformation of the individual consciousness by lift-
ing it to a level above its own particularity, to the level
of universality through a detachment from the particular, to a level which is akin to the universality of the
Divine Consciousness. Freedom lies in this universality.
. . . Now that the world is becoming consciously one
and cultures are influencing and interpenetrating each
other, a set of values common to men of all cultures
ought to be and can be discovered. . . . (P. T. Raju,
"On a Hierarchy of Values Common to All Cultures,"
*Hyphen Annual* [Sept., 1959], pp. 59-62.)

These selections from a well-conceived and well-
argued essay by Professor P. T. Raju of Jodhpur fail
to do justice to the reasonableness of his point of
view. But they at least express his faith, which is

shared by many the world over, though their ways of defending this faith may vary considerably in style and in philosophy. As expressed by Professor Raju, this is more than a confession of faith. It appears to him to be the logical implication of two facts: (1) that there is a human species; (2) that there is a human construction called civilization in which all human cultures participate and towards the realization of which they converge as they become better acquainted with each other and with the art of civilization.

Now, I, for one, would confess that I share his belief that there is a process in which all mankind is involved, a creative process which is becoming increasingly conscious and organized, and which might as well be called the universal human art of civilization. Let others call it by other names, the important fact is the fact of increasing cultural interpenetration and reciprocity of influence. In the general art of improving human life, the trials and errors of innumerable societies, past, present, and future, are all contributing values and value judgments; and these values and evaluations are becoming increasingly intercultural and transcultural. In short, there is now a substantial basis of fact and achievement to make the term "human civilization" mean something concrete. I know there are sceptics who smile at this. I know there are anthropologists who ask us please not to complicate the science of various cultures by dragging in the useless term "civilization," as though it had no plural. And I know that there are moralists who will accuse me of preaching a superficial and disastrous syncretism. "Syncretism" is among theologians the unforgiveable sin, for they conceive it to be an attempt to create an interfaith to take the place of all genuine faiths.

Neither Professor Raju nor I am guilty of any such intentions. There can be cultural diversity and relativity, world without end, so far as we are concerned. The more the better, I should say. What those of us who believe in such an enterprise as morals-for-mankind wish to assert is that no human creations are to be conceived as alien to mankind's growing, cooperative effort to improve the general conditions of human life. The humanists of the Renaissance had a Latin phrase for this idea. The idea is not new, but it is becoming increasingly meaningful.

But where Professor Raju and I differ, and each of us has allies in our difference, is that Professor Raju thinks it is meaningless to use such a term as "improve" as I have just used it, unless "improvement" can be defined in terms of a hierarchy of basic values.

This seems a rational position to take and you will probably agree that he has the better logic in the argument. If "improvement" or "progress" and their synonyms have no definite goal, it is meaningless, you will conclude, to say that there is a single process of creation in which all mankind cooperates. No one can know whether he is making progress until he knows where he intends to go. And similarly, you say, if men are making cooperative progress, they must be working for common values.

Despite the apparent reasonableness of this point of view, I think the facts do not justify it. Basic values are actually more diversified than this theory allows, and they do not form a hierarchy. In a concrete situation several values may arrange themselves neatly as higher and lower on a scale which may be fairly objective or standardized. But such local and temporary scales do not remain fixed eternally. Even if values were eternal or ultimate, for which there is little evidence, the relations among them would shift from situation to situation. The scales are weighted differently for different circumstances, and the attempts to construct absolute or ultimate hierarchies have seldom endured much longer than those who from time to time construct such scales. In sober fact, no human being has enough foresight to

see to the end or goal of civilization. The beginnings
of history are obscure enough. Who can tell where
and how mankind will find its culmination?

The obvious reply might be that all men must at
least *believe* in progress or improvement. But this
begs the question. Progress and improvement are
not themselves values. They are the process in which
values find their context or field of operation. All
men might be making progress without all going in
the same direction. Who knows in which direction
universal progress leads? Who knows whether progress is linear or cyclical or dialectical or zigzag? The
path of progress may not be straight and narrow at
all, and it need not have a definable end or culmi-
nate in the realization of a fixed ideal. It is common
practice among modern philosophers to say, with
Professor Raju, that progress is the increasing realization of freedom. I would agree that without freedom in some sense, progress would be meaningless.
Freedom is in the air which civilization breathes. It
is one of the means or conditions of progress rather
than its end. When conceived as the ultimate goal it
is apt to lose all concrete meaning, and to become
once more as abstract as it was in Hegel's philosophy
of history. When freedom is spelled out into four or
five freedoms, it immediately becomes dated and

localized in some historical new deal or particular emancipation.

I know that these few objections constitute no adequate refutation of Professor Raju's faith in a hierarchy of values, but I hope they are sufficient to suggest that the logic of this faith is not as self-evident as it seems at first sight. In particular, I hope they are sufficient to make us doubtful about resting our whole case for a morality for mankind on our supposed ability to discern the ultimate values toward which humanity is moving.

For myself, I find it impossible to build a universal ethics on either natural law at the beginning or ultimate values at the end of civilization. We find ourselves at sea, in fairly deep water, far from either shore; we may not be in the middle of history, but it usually seems like the middle to those who try to find their bearings. We know little about where we began and less about where we shall end. What guidance we can get, then, must be along the way, trusting to favorable winds and currents, avoiding circular motion or mere drifting, even though our exploration is into the unknown. Whatever morals we create to keep us together on the journey will be a traveler's code, a plan for staying together in all sorts of weather, though we are without a complete map for the trip. Since I have drifted into marine rhetoric, I might better quote the master moralist for mariners, Herman Melville:

> Oh, shipmates and world-mates, all round! We the people suffer many abuses. . . . In vain from Lieutenants do we appeal to the Captain; in vain—while on board our world-frigate—to the indefinite Navy Commissioners, so far out of sight aloft. Yet the worst of our evils we blindly inflict upon ourselves; our officers can not relieve them, even if they would. From the last ills no being can save another; therein each man must be his own savior. . . . Let us not mutiny. . . . (*White Jacket*.)

After this discouraging digression into theoretical world-ethics, let us return to the more practical aspects of a science of ethics and ask what kinds of bonds there are which even now make men aware that their co-existence is more than physical, and which may serve as a strong enough network of common interests to serve mankind in its civilizing efforts. I would rely on three kinds of such bonds as being available (and possibly availing) for a worldwide community: common needs, reciprocal obligations, and liberal exchanges.

1. *Common Needs:*

It is important to distinguish between common laws, common needs, and common goals or values.

Needs are intermediate between beginnings and ends, between principles and values. Needs are means, and they may be shared, when neither principles nor ends are shared. The same means, health, for example, may be used for a variety of ends and are not derived from common norms of right and wrong. Life, liberty, health, home, work, education, recreation, pursuit of happiness—and you may add whatever else is commonly included under elementary necessities for civilization. In addition to such personal needs there are community needs: water supply, transportation, power and light, basic communication mechanisms, public sanitation, basic medical services, schools, basic arts of expression. Some such group of commonplace essentials for social life would constitute a minimum for decent living. There would be considerable variation in the precise meaning of each in different climates, different cultures, different institutions. Foods vary, homes vary, means of transportation and communication vary, etc. Hence by "common needs," we cannot mean "identical needs." And we cannot infer that the golden rule should apply literally, that we should treat all as we wish to be treated. Where tastes, cultures, standards vary, it would be foolish as well as immoral to treat all according to our own tastes and needs. If each person thought it his duty to see to it that all were supplied with what he himself needed, there would be absolute chaos. The golden rule is not golden when applied thus literally. Nor should we apply to needs the traditional doctrine of natural rights, and claim that all men have a right to what they need. All men need health, but they cannot demand it as a right; all men need friends, but the love of friends cannot be obtained on demand as a right. Common needs are different from natural rights, and exist obviously whether there are any natural rights or not. The recognition of common or basic needs should not be confused with natural rights or natural needs. Certain moralists (Adam Smith, for example) have attempted to define man's "natural" needs but this is too speculative a proposition, and is usually abandoned, as it was by Adam Smith himself. Needs are difficult enough to define without adding the still vaguer qualification, "natural." Needs are commonly recognized by all, though no two persons have the same needs. It is this common readiness to distinguish between needs and desires, between necessities and luxuries, that provides a possible basis for general understanding among men. Few will insist that all men are equal and have equal needs. And few are

sanguine enough to let each person name his own
needs. If needs were Cadillacs, beggars would drive.
We all know that most men think they need more
than they do need. On the other hand, we all know
of persons who are not sufficiently conscious of their
needs. Consciousness of needs is no adequate measure of real needs. Let us admit, without dispute,
that needs cannot be perfectly standardized and certainly not made uniform for all mankind. In other
words, let us not assume that common needs are
common in the sense of being uniform. What we
mean by this phrase is that there should be a common concern among men of all cultures to give the
satisfaction of needs priority over other types of satisfaction when it comes to policies of public morals.
That all men should have what they really need
should be a public concern everywhere. It may very
well be physically impossible to meet all needs, but
that should not excuse us from being concerned
whenever men are frustrated by not getting what
they need. *Misery anywhere should be a moral concern everywhere.* You will note that I am emphasiz-
ing moral concern here; this dimension of morality,
which I call "concern," is to be distinguished from
the dimension of rights and duties, for not all matters of concern are matters of obligation. What I am

urging here is simply that all men should have an intelligent interest in and moral concern for the needs of all men. This is one aspect of conscientiousness for mankind.

## 2. *Reciprocal Obligations:*

Now we turn to the aspect of obligation, of rights and duties. Here morality becomes more formal and more definite. A general sense of right or duty or responsibility is worth little. When everybody is responsible, no one is. For a long time moralists have preached humanitarianism, and during the Enlightenment there were many religious societies which called themselves "Theophilanthropist." To cultivate a love for mankind is certainly a virtue and a civic virtue. But now I am not preaching virtue. I have more specific obligations in mind. To make morals for mankind effective in action, not merely in sentiment, we must be able to claim rights and demand performances that have practical meaning and that involve definite responsibilities for specified persons or groups. Some of these carry only the sanctions of approval or disapproval; others have legal sanctions behind them. In either case they are the most central and serious matters of conscience. For obligations must have binding power; without some

definite moral bonds among all men, we are still far
from a human community.

The first, most obvious and most general obligation is to refrain from inhumanity. In many ways recently man's inhumanity to man has been called
forcibly to everyone's attention. We have so many
clear cases of inhumanity before us that we cannot
excuse indifference on the ground that "inhumanity" is too vague a term. It is much more definite
than "humanity" and "humanitarianism." Even if
we may not be able to define it to a lawyer's satisfaction, there are many concrete varieties of inhumanity which are recognized as criminal in the public
conscience.

The foremost case is the threat our governments
hold, not against each other but against all humanity, to blow up everything. Certainly, all men should
hold their governments responsible, whether governments are responsible to their peoples or not, to refrain from such an act of diabolical inhumanity.
This is neither peace nor war in which we are living.
It is carrying intimidation for the sake of bargaining
power to insane lengths. Carrying out the threat
would not be war, but merely complete ruin. To use
megaton explosive devices as instruments of so-called
negotiation is an inhuman form of bargaining. And

I agree wholeheartedly with Thomas Murray, formerly of the Atomic Energy Commission, that the first obligation our governments owe to mankind is to initiate at once an "orderly destruction on a matching basis of existing megaton weapons under international supervision." "International politics perishes as an art if power is allowed to suffer moral degradation and become mere violence, destructive of the very idea of force and of law, too." There must be an "end to the era of terror and the threat of unlimited violence." (*Los Angeles Times,* February 14, 1960.)

The buzz-bombs sent into England during the last war were an atrocity. Hiroshima was an atrocity. The present "era of terror" is an atrocious form of inhumanity. No government can claim that its people sanction such brutality and it is to humanity as a whole that any government owes it to desist from such terrorism. This is the first of all obligations to mankind.

The second is to make peace by civilized forms of negotiation. Peace must be made piecemeal (pardon the pun) by an arduous process of conciliatory handling of international conflicts. Mankind may never be at peace, but the obligation to seek peace is universal and urgent. The general obligation which lies

on governments and individuals alike is to cultivate
habits of peaceful conduct. The specific rules or
principles of such conduct have never been formulated better, so it seems to me, than by Thomas
Hobbes in his *Leviathan*. Living in a time of terror, as
we do, he formulated his "articles of peace" so care-
fully that they have a universal application today as
well as in the days of the British Commonwealth under Cromwell, when he formulated them. He called
them "natural laws" of reason as well as "articles of
peace." But he clearly justified them not by principles of natural law but as conduct necessary to make
peace. Here are his ten commandments:

(1) Every man ought to seek peace, for in a condition where every man can injure any man
as he pleases there can be no security, and
everyone seeks security both by necessity of
his nature and by natural right.

(2) Every man, if he fails to find peace, should
defend himself as best he can in war.

(3) Every man should renounce his right to defend himself in so far as all agree to renounce
their rights to the extent they find it necessary for peace.

(4) If men make such agreements, they must
perform what they promise. This law is the

fountain and origin of justice, for the breach of a covenant is unjust, and what is not unjust is just.

(5) If a man offers peace without covenant, the man that receives should see to it that the giver has no reasonable ground for repenting of his good will. For no man gives voluntarily unless he expects good to come of it for himself and if this expectation is frustrated there is an end of benevolence, trust, and peace. This is the law of Gratitude.

(6) Every man should strive to accommodate himself to the rest, for if a man through hardness of heart strive to retain those things which are superfluous to him but necessary to others, he is guilty of the struggle which naturally follows upon such unsociableness and stubbornness.

(7) Punishments must not be based on the evil past, but on the future security and peace. Revenge without profit is cruelty, and such vainglory is contrary to reason, since it tends toward war.

(8) No man by deed, word, countenance, or gesture should declare hatred or contempt of another, for all signs of hatred or contempt provoke to fight.

(9) Every man should acknowledge others as equals and not reserve to himself any right which he is not content should be reserved to anyone of the rest, for man will not enter into conditions of peace except on equal terms.

(10) Any man who is trusted to judge between man and man must judge equitably, for partial judgment is a cause of conflict.

These rules have a Puritan rigor, but they also have a rigorous logic. Let no man underestimate the severity of the obligations all must live up to, if all men are to become neighbors. Neither Hobbes nor I speak of brotherhood; it is neighborliness we are aiming at when we speak of morals suitable for mankind.

3. *Liberal Exchanges:*

Common needs and obligations will go unheeded, if there is no sharing of other interests. Mankind cannot live on morals alone, for morality is after all an effort to create an orderly environment for other arts and diversified interests. So long as men are culturally isolated, they may respect each other formally at a distance, but they will remain strangers. Unless there is some personal acquaintance and an actual

sharing of problems and faiths, arts and achieve-
ments, it is idle to think of mankind as more than a
somber union of debtors and creditors who meet
only in an office to transact unpleasant business.

It is less than seventy years ago that F. H. Bradley,
a meticulous moralist, wrote:

> We cannot argue in general from civic to international
> morality, and in particular we cannot transport the
> duty of self-sacrifice unaltered into the world at large.
> A man owes a debt to his country, but a nation may
> feel it owes nothing to some other nation. Duty to one's
> neighbor remains, but then who is one's neighbor?
> Within the community he is another representative of
> the same ideas, and I can believe, when I sacrifice my-
> self, that my life survives in the whole, and that the
> common spirit gains by my loss. Can a state say this of
> a neighbour alien in race and alien in ideas? Or may
> not self-sacrifice bring here no advantage, and but re-
> sult in fruitless waste?
>
> There is, of course, no international morality. . . .
> And it is doubtful if international law can be said
> really to exist. . . . International courts seem hardly
> possible; they could not be presumed to be always rep-
> resentative or even disinterested. . . . Outside the state
> there is no good. ("The Limits of Individual and Na-
> tional Self-Sacrifice," *International Journal of Ethics,* V
> [1894], pp. 19-22, *passim.*)

Bradley was trying to be a realistic idealist; he little dreamed that within so short a time international institutions which he thought impossible would be operating successfully. It is ironical that he published these nationalistic sentiments in the *International Journal of Ethics*! Even as his essay went to press, international agencies were beginning to undermine the truth of his contentions. What made this revolution in morals possible was the revolution in the instruments of intercultural communication and exchanges, translations and travel. Mankind is now physically able to get acquainted with itself. On the progress of this process of getting acquainted all over the earth depends the vitality of a world-wide neighborliness. In a typical modern community it is not necessary that neighbors be friends or brothers. They may have very different interests and standards, but they care enough about each other to wonder what these various interests and standards are, and to cooperate in providing public utilities and personal needs. Such neighborly relations are now possible on a world-wide scale. In fact, they are urgent.

Several years ago a small group of us Western philosophers met in Asia with a small group of Asian philosophers to discuss the obligations which the

peoples of the earth owe each other. We were not
discussing international relations in the political
sense, nor foreign policies; we wondered whether we
could agree on the principles of intercultural obligations. One or two of the Asian philosophers sug-
gested at once that there are needy peoples and peoples with surpluses. They said, very frankly, according to our ethics you owe us your surpluses. Somewhat amazed, we asked, "Do you claim a moral right
to our surpluses?" "No," they replied, "we do not
think in terms of rights; we prefer to think of obligations. These are your obligations. Our obligation is
not to beg for your surpluses but to learn to live a
life of suffering." The other Asians, however, inter-
rupted what might have become an acrimonious debate by maintaining a prior obligation which both
East and West shared. I quote their words:

> The general principle underlying such intercultural
> obligations is: there must be (as a duty) enough con-
> sideration for, and interest in neighboring cultures to
> keep the door open for communications. Though no
> amount of active exchange and communication can be
> morally prescribed among peoples, there must be a
> maintenance of institutional means of exchange and
> communications, so that voluntary co-operation, if it
> exists, is not frustrated by physical obstacles or isola-
> tion. . . . There are many non-governmental agencies

on whom the chief responsibility rests for maintaining an open door and effective instruments for actively promoting international understanding, reciprocal respect, cultural exchanges, and other services, credits, and gifts. (*Human Relations and International Obligations, A Symposium,* ed. N. A. Nikam, Indian Philosophical Congress, 1956, pp. 302-303.)

It is this aspect of a morality embracing mankind that I wish to emphasize in closing. There is a context of "voluntary co-operation" which is necessary to the effective operation of moral concerns and obligations. Without a certain amount of communication, exchange, reciprocal interest, it is in vain to expect unneighborly peoples to acknowledge their obligations or to show intelligent concern. Prior to foreign aid comes an attempt not to be foreigners. And in this attitude of "keeping the door open," the nonpolitical interests and organizations must take the lead. A universal neighborliness does not imply a "love" of all mankind nor even a respect for the dignity of every man. Love and respect are later developments. Concerns, duties, and neighborliness come first, and the first of these three is neighborliness. Love begins at home, but conscience should not be so exclusive. Morality is seriously defective until it includes mankind, not only on scientific principle but also in actual behavior.